PHILLIPS TRADITIONAL SCHOOL

America's Early Settlers

Moments in History

by Shirley Jordan

Perfection Learning®

Cover and Book Design: Alan D. Stanley

About the Author

Shirley Jordan is a retired elementary school teacher and principal. Currently a lecturer in the teacher-training program at California State University, Fullerton, California, she sees exciting things happening in the world of social studies. Shirley loves to travel—with a preference for sites important to U.S. history.

She has had more than 50 travel articles published in recent years. It was through her travels that she became interested in "moments in history," those ironic and little-known stories that make one exclaim, "I didn't know that!" Such stories are woven throughout her books.

Image credits: Art Today pp. 4, 5, 7, 8, 9, 11, 12, 13, 14, 15, 16, 17, 18, 20, 21, 23, 25, 26, 28, 30, 31, 34, 35, 38, 45, 46, 48, 50, 51 bottom, 52, 53, 54 top, 55, 56, 57, 58, 59, cover; Corbis pp. 10, 39; Corbis-Bettmann p. 51 top; Corbis-Francis G. Mayer p. 54 bottom; Corbis-G.E. Kidder Smith p. 36; Corel pp. 29, 47, 60

Text © 2000 by Perfection Learning® Corporation.
All rights reserved. No part of this book may be used or reproduced in any manner whatsoever without written permission from the publisher.
Printed in the United States of America. For information, contact Perfection Learning® Corporation, 1000 North Second Avenue, P.O. Box 500, Logan, Iowa 51546-0500.
Tel: 1-800-831-4190 • Fax: 1-712-644-2392
Paperback ISBN 0-7891-5142-1
Cover Craft® ISBN 0-7807-9309-9

Table of Contents

A Timeline of Important Events. 4

Chapter 1. America's Earliest Settlers 6

Chapter 2. The English Come to North America 8

Chapter 3. The Colony at Jamestown 12

Chapter 4. An Escape from England 18

Chapter 5. A New Start in Holland 23

Chapter 6. A Captain Prepares His Ship. 27

Chapter 7. The Voyage Is Delayed 31

Chapter 8. Aboard the *Mayflower* 33

Chapter 9. The Settlers Find New Friends 36

Chapter 10. Other Settlers Come to the New World . . . 41

Chapter 11. The Craftsmen Among the Settlers 44

Chapter 12. Governor Winthrop's Wonderful Tool . . . 48

Chapter 13. The People Spread to New Settlements . . . 50

Chapter 14. The Many Journeys of Plymouth Rock . . . 57

Glossary 61

Index 63

A Timeline of Important Events

Before Recorded Time	Men and women walk across huge ice fields. They cross from Siberia in Russia to Alaska. Then they **migrate** south.
1564	French Huguenots found a colony in what is now Florida. It lasts one year.
1565	Spaniard Pedro de Avilés founds St. Augustine, Florida.
1585	A small group of Englishmen begin a settlement on Roanoke Island, Virginia.
1607	Three ships sent by the London Company land in Virginia. Captain John Smith and the others found Jamestown. It is the first permanent English settlement in America.
	That same year, the Puritans leave England and go to Holland. They seek freedom of religion.
1608	French explorer Samuel de Champlain founds a settlement in Quebec on the St. Lawrence River.
1609	Henry Hudson sails up the Hudson River. He claims its valley for the Dutch.
	Champlain explores the rivers in present-day Maine and sails south to Cape Cod. The French claim these lands. But they send no settlers.
1609/1610	Spaniards found Santa Fe, New Mexico.
1612	The English settlers plant tobacco in Virginia for the first time.

4

1614	In Jamestown, Pocahontas marries settler John Rolfe.
1620	The Puritans return to England from Holland. They and other English families prepare to sail to the New World.
	Plymouth Colony settled by those on the *Mayflower*.
	The Mayflower Compact signed.
1621	Massasoit, leader of the Wampanoag Indians, makes peace with the Pilgrims at Plymouth.
1622	Opechancanough leads a great massacre of the English settlers around Jamestown.
1626	The Dutch buy Manhattan Island from the Indians for about $24.
1630	During the next ten years, the Puritans spread through the Massachusetts Bay Colony and beyond.
1634	Lord Calvert founds Maryland.
1636	Roger Williams founds Rhode Island.
	Thomas Hooker moves to Connecticut.
1638	Anne Hutchinson leads her followers to Rhode Island.
1664	The English capture New Amsterdam and rename it New York.
1667	The first group of English Quakers comes to America.
1681	William Penn founds Pennsylvania.
1693	Witchcraft trials are held in Salem, Massachusetts.
1697	French settlers come to the Louisiana Territory claimed by La Salle.
1699	Williamsburg becomes capital of Virginia.
1732	James Oglethorpe founds Georgia.

Chapter 1

America's Earliest Settlers

Before the journeys of the Vikings and Columbus there were settlers in North America. Most historians agree that these men and women walked across huge ice fields. They came from Siberia, Russia. They walked across Alaska. Then these settlers moved south. They passed through what are now Canada and the United States. This happened hundreds, perhaps thousands, of years ago.

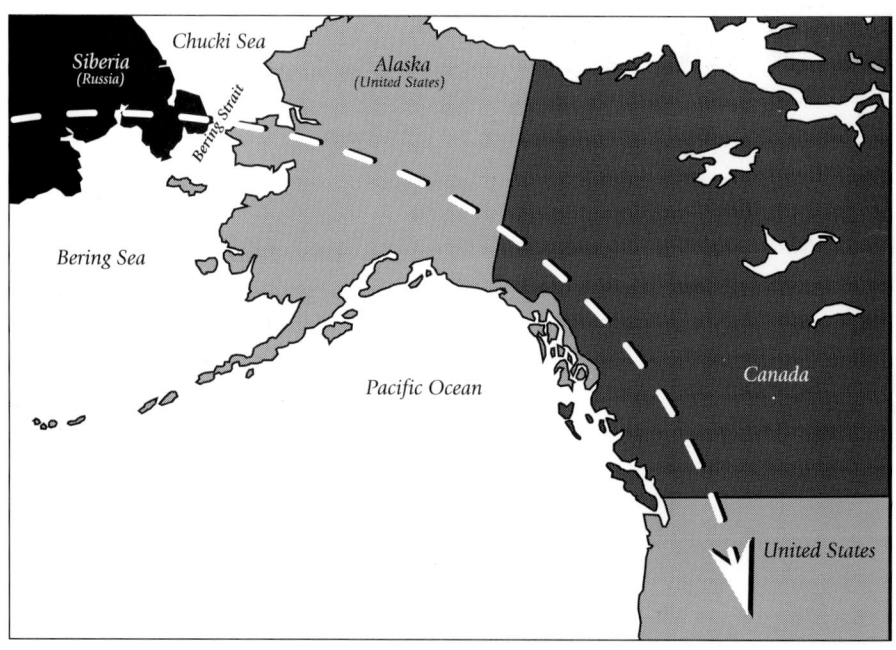

Early explorers from Europe, like Columbus, came to America. They thought they had reached the Indies. So they called these **native** people *Indians*. Today, we know them as Native Americans.

These early Native Americans were scattered all over the Americas. They had their own traditions and ways of living. Historians have found ruins of their huge pyramids. Some tribes had apartment-house communities with as many as 800 rooms.

These first settlers used fire for cooking and for warmth in winter. In North America, many of them smeared their bodies with fatty grease taken from bears they had killed. This helped keep their bodies warm. But it made their skin look red.

Some Native Americans worked with metal. And they had a fine system of **irrigation.** This was important for growing corn, squash, and beans.

These early Americans had no written language. And the languages they spoke were different from tribe to tribe. So they could not communicate and interact. Therefore, the tribes did not join together into large communities. By the time Columbus reached the New World, 500 small tribes were scattered across America.

Chapter 2

The English Come to North America

More than 400 years ago, Englishmen first tried to settle in America. There were many reasons. For English rulers like Queen Elizabeth I and then King James I, a colony in America would increase trade.

And there would be safe, friendly harbors for English ships. These were needed because of continuing wars with the Spanish **Armada.**

Queen Elizabeth I

The Spanish were already in the New World. They had settled a place we now call Florida. They were far south of where the English wanted to go.

London businessmen were interested in America too. Exciting stories were coming back from across the sea. They told of gold, silver, and precious jewels.

These stories said riches were just lying around on the shores of North America. **Investors** wanted to send others to bring back the riches.

8

For the common person, America was a place a family could start a whole new life. Great stretches of land were waiting. A farmer and his family could do well there.

The Lost Colony at Roanoke Island

On April 9, 1585, around 108 men sailed from England. They were sent by Sir Walter Raleigh. This explorer and businessman had made an earlier discovery voyage to the New World.

Raleigh sent the Englishmen to settle a special area he had explored. He called it Roanoke Island. The island was just off the shore of a land called Virginia.

Virginia was a huge piece of land at that time. It was much bigger than the state of Virginia is today. Raleigh's Virginia territory included what are now the states of Pennsylvania and North Carolina.

Did Raleigh want a base from which to rob the Spanish ships to the south? Did he want a friendly harbor for the English navy when it fought the Spanish?

He didn't get either one.

The men he'd sent to Roanoke missed their families. Crops grew poorly. And the Indians frightened them. They always seemed to be watching what the settlers did.

After the Englishmen had been there a year, the great explorer Sir Francis Drake stopped at Roanoke Island. The tired, hungry settlers rushed to Drake's ships. Crowding on board, they sailed back to London.

A popular story is told about Raleigh. Some people said he once placed his coat over a puddle. He did this so Queen Elizabeth I could walk on it and not get her feet muddy and wet. Whether this happened or not, we do know that the queen was a good friend to Raleigh.

Roanoke in the Indian language meant "shell money."

9

Raleigh didn't give up. He sent another group. But these people also returned home as soon as possible. All returned except 15 hardy members of that second party. Those few decided to stay.

In 1587, a third group sailed from England. They were bound for Roanoke. There were 117 settlers. And this time there were some families. With the respected English captain John White were 91 men, 17 women, and 9 children.

It was a sad arrival. The new settlers found no sign of the 15 men who had stayed at Roanoke. John White had hoped for better news.

Just 27 days after the landing on August 18, a baby girl was born. Virginia Dare was the first English child born on the American continent. John White was proud and excited. This newest member of the settlement was his grandchild.

Supplies soon ran low. The few crops the English settlers planted did not grow well. Winter would come soon. And they were not well prepared.

So John White and a few crewmen prepared their ship. They had to sail home and bring back a shipload of food.

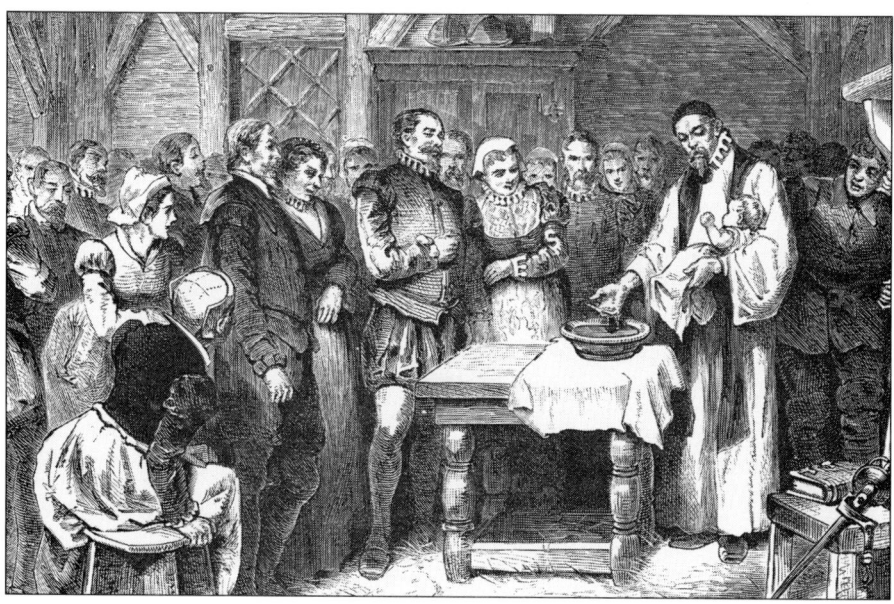

The baptism of Virginia Dare

10

Captain White and his men reached England after two months at sea. The war between the English and Spanish navies was at its worst. No ship was safe upon the seas. Even if the war ended, White would need time to raise money for supplies.

By the time White returned to the New World, it was 1590. He had been gone from Roanoke almost three years.

At last, he and his ship filled with supplies landed at Roanoke Island. Everything there was very quiet. No one came to greet the ship.

Fearfully, White and others searched the beach and settlement. Not a single person remained.

The only trace of the 117 settlers and White's three-year-old grandchild was a single word carved on a tree: C R O A T O A N.

What could this mean?

Were the settlers killed by Indians? Did they marry into the Indian tribes in the area? If they starved, why was there no sign of their last days?

The settlement on Roanoke Island was lost forever. The mystery remains today.

Chapter 3

The Colony at Jamestown

Battles to control the seas continued for years. But in 1588, England finally conquered the Spanish Armada. Now English adventurers felt bold when crossing the Atlantic Ocean.

Now was the time for settlements. And settlements could mean riches for those who invested their money.

Rich men began to form exploration companies. The king awarded them land in the New World. These men agreed to buy supplies and send ships. But they needed settlers to make the trip.

On the very last day of 1606, a group of 104 English men and boys gathered on an English dock. Bobbing in the harbor were three small ships: the *Susan Constant,* the *Godspeed,* and the *Discovery.* An organization known as the London Company was sending these men to the New World.

No women were along on this journey. Seventy-four of the men were wealthy landholders. Used to power and an easy life, they dressed in their best clothes for the trip. They expected others to wait on them.

Only 20 of those boarding the ships were common laborers. With them were four carpenters, one blacksmith, one sail maker, and four young boys. These 30 men and boys would do the heavy work in the new colony.

The journey was a cruel one. The winter weather beat upon the frail vessels. For four months, the three small ships rolled and tossed across the wide Atlantic Ocean.

The men missed their families. And they were frightened. Would they ever arrive in the New World alive?

At last, the long struggle was over. The three ships limped into the fine bay we now know as the Chesapeake. Then they sailed inland. They traveled up a gentle river they named the James, after their king.

For three weeks, they searched along 60 miles of the river. Where should they land? On May 14, 1607, they chose a small **peninsula** on the river.

King James I

The place turned out to be a poor choice. Jamestown, named for the English king, was swampy. The water was not pure enough to drink. And the weather was much colder than they had expected in this new land.

Weak from their long trip at sea, many men fell ill. Soon they burned with the fevers of **malaria, pneumonia,** and **dysentery.**

13

Here is a journal that could have been written by one of the carpenters.

June 10, 1607

We have been here at Jamestown for almost a month now. Work on the settlement is going slowly. Many are sick. Others can't decide what to do first. If we did not have fine leaders like Captain Christopher Newport and Captain John Smith, we would be done for.

Every day men search for gold. They dig and dig. Then they pour water over the piles of dirt. They sort through the washed soil. But so far no one has found even the smallest piece of shiny gold.

Captain John Smith

King James promised we would all be paid for coming to Virginia. Each week our pay is written in the book. But the king has not said who is to do the work.

Most of the rich gentlemen have never had to labor. They just sit about for hours in their fancy clothes. They seem to like to watch the carpenters and laborers do the work. It's wrong for all of us to be paid the same!

No one knows much about growing food. The grape plants we brought did not do well at all. But the Indians gave us some corn. That is growing now.

Still, the gentlemen don't want to get their hands dirty. They won't plant crops, build homes, or hunt for food.

With so many sick, we are kept busy burying the dead. The rich men won't help with the grave digging either.

We never know what the Indians will do. Sometimes they seem ready to attack us. And twice they have threatened to kill John Smith. But at other times they treat us like brothers.

Pocahontas, Chief Powhatan's young daughter, is our friend. She saved John Smith. Just as the Indians were ready to cut off his head, she put her head on top of his. Her surprised father stopped the killing and let Captain Smith go free.

Where will all this lead?

October 10, 1607

House building is slow. It is hard to see how warm shelters can be ready by winter. Each cold night I dream of home.

But now, I think God has smiled upon us. The Indians saw how few men were actually working on the houses. They came and showed us how to build a different kind of home quickly.

John Smith wrote about Pocahontas saving his life after he returned to England. Some historians don't believe this story. They ask questions such as why would a young girl who didn't know Captain Smith save his life. They think he wrote this story to make people think he was a hero.

First we tie a few long sapling branches together at one end. Then we wrap animal hides around the branches to make a kind of tent. The Indians call these **wigwams.** With a fire inside, they are warm and dry in bad weather.

December 20, 1607

The long winter drags on. There is little food left. Some men planted nothing. They were afraid the Indians would come to raid their homes while they worked in the fields.

As soon as the snows melt, we will begin building real houses. How I would welcome a **wattle-and-daub** house like we had in England! I will make a timber frame and add wooden wattles. Then I'll daub them with the rich mud of our

riverbank. We have a good supply of straw for the roofs too.

15

Starvation, bad weather, and diseases are taking more of our people. Out of the 104 who arrived last April, only 38 of us are left.

January 10, 1608

Something wonderful has happened.

A ship filled with supplies arrived to save us. And it brought many more settlers.

How shocked the newcomers were at our weak condition. They thought we would have many crops from our land too.

We are happy to have more Englishmen here. But still we do not have enough food to feed everyone well.

July 10, 1609

Captain John Smith has been in charge of the colony for a year now. When he took over, he made new rules. Now everyone must work. He said, "He that will not work shall not eat." What a shock that was to the rich and powerful men who came here to find gold!

Now our hearts are heavy, though. Captain Smith has had a terrible accident. A spark set fire to his gunpowder pouch. It blew up and set fire to his red beard. He was badly burned. After a week, he is no better. Tomorrow a ship will take him back to England.

How we shall all miss our leader!

After John Smith left Jamestown, there were both good and bad times.

That first winter, 1609–1610, was an especially cruel one. Historians call it "The Starving Time."

The Indians became unfriendly. Too many people wanted their land.

Settlers didn't dare go outside their fences to hunt. It was even dangerous to leave home to search for firewood.

The desperate Englishmen ate dogs, rats, and mice. Only about 60 settlers made it through that winter.

In June, 300 new settlers arrived with supplies. And with them came a strong leader. He was Lord De la Warr. (The state of Delaware would later be named for him.) He made firm rules. Anyone who did not obey was punished. Some settlers were unhappy about his rules. They ran away and found ships to take them home to England.

In 1612, one of the colonists, John Rolfe, found a way to grow a mild tobacco that Englishmen liked. The seeds came from the island of Trinidad near South America. Now with tobacco, the settlers had a crop that would bring them some money.

And in 1614, John Rolfe married Pocahontas. This brought peace to the settlement. Jamestown continued to grow.

But in 1622, the Indians became unhappy again. Too many Englishmen had come. They were taking all the best lands. There were few animals left in the hunting grounds. There were few fish in the fishing grounds.

Powhatan had died in 1618. The chief who followed him was Opechancanough. He did not like the white men. In March 1622, the Indians attacked and killed 347 settlers.

The settlement struggled to survive. In 1644, another Indian attack claimed 500 men, women, and children. And in 1676 and in 1698, terrible fires burned most of the town. Finally, the unhappy settlers gave up. They moved their government to the nearby town of Williamsburg.

17

Chapter 4

An Escape from England

It was 1607, the same year the *Susan Constant, Godspeed,* and *Discovery* carried the Jamestown settlers to the New World. Another group of English men and women were about to set out in a different direction.

These Englishmen were the **Puritans.** And in 1607, being a Puritan was dangerous. England's King James wanted everyone to attend the powerful Church of England. But William Bradford, William Brewster, and their friends wanted to choose their own way to worship God.

Puritans believed in simple prayers and hymn singing. In fact, they spent all day Sunday in church. People knew them for their pure thoughts and ideas. That's how they had come to be called "Puritans."

William Bradford

One day in 1607, young Bradford and his friends looked out to sea. A ship was anchored not far from shore. As the men watched, a rowboat was lowered from the larger vessel. It moved toward them. Soon they would escape.

Freedom seemed closer now. But first, the 51 Puritans from the village of Scrooby must board that ship. Then they'd leave England behind them.

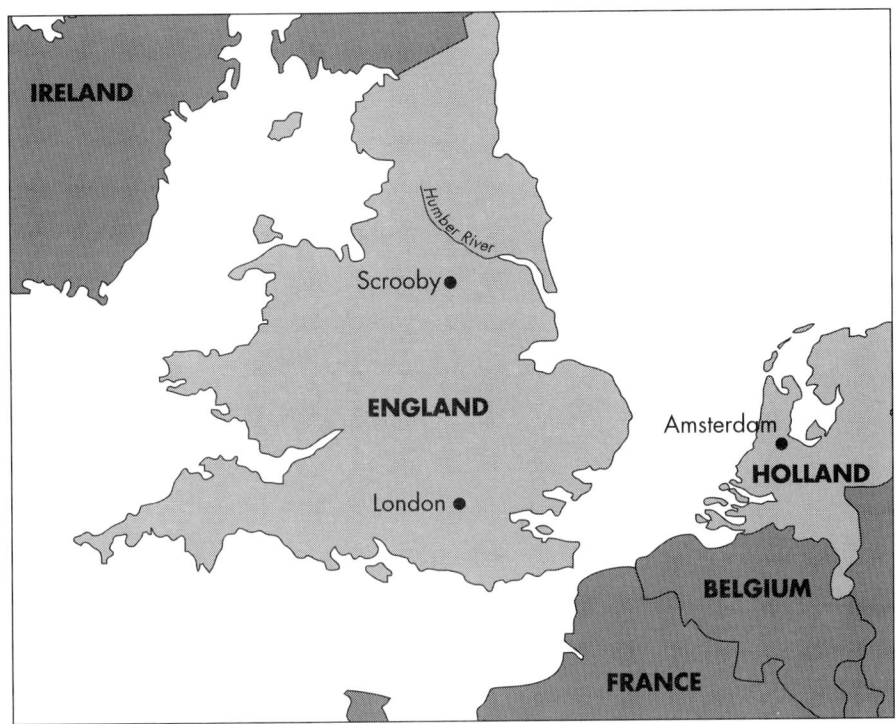

William Bradford waited for the small rowboat. He thought about what had happened the summer before in 1606. His family and about 50 others had tried to escape from England to Holland. The Dutch people would let each family worship as it chose.

The Puritans had hired a captain to sail them to Holland. But instead, he did a terrible thing. He took their money and told the king's soldiers about the plan. It was against the law to leave England without permission.

Before they could sail away, the ship was stopped by boatloads of the king's soldiers. They rushed on board. Then they forced the Puritans to return to their homes in Scrooby.

In the months that followed, the Puritans kept their prayer meetings and hymn sings secret. Anyone in town might be a spy.

Now it was spring again. Once more they planned an escape to Holland. The men had walked for 40 miles. It had taken many days to reach England's shore. Again they waited for a ship.

19

Leaving their homes in Scrooby had not been easy. There was only one small boat to take them to the coast. It was flat like a barge and had sails. Such a boat was meant to sail on rivers.

The boat held only the women and children and a few pieces of furniture. Could they get away secretly? Everyone had to be very quiet. They hid under canvas covers.

The Puritans hired some men to pole the barge down one stream after another. Finally, they reached the place where the Humber River flowed into the sea.

Now, standing on the shore, Will Bradford sensed something was wrong. Where were the women and children? They should have arrived earlier—long before the men and boys.

Perhaps, he thought, our families are already on board the Dutch ship.

But this was not the case. The women and children had reached the coast too quickly. They arrived a full day early. They feared they might be found by the king's soldiers. So the families huddled in the small vessel.

The sea grew rough. The mothers and children became seasick. At last, they begged the barge workers to use their poles and move the vessel into a small creek where the water was quiet.

This was a mistake. As the tide went out, the barge became firmly stuck in the mud of the creek. It wouldn't move an inch!

In the morning, the Dutch ship arrived. The captain saw the problem. He sailed as near to the land as he could. But the women and children had no way to get to the ship. Only the tide could set them free.

While he waited for the tide, the Dutch captain saw the Puritan men and boys arrive on shore. He would load them first. Soon a boatload, including Will Bradford, was rowed out to the sailing ship.

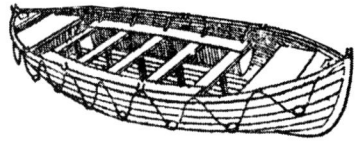

The Dutch sailors in the rowboat spoke only their own language. So some of the Puritan men were on board before the English-speaking captain pointed out the stuck barge back on shore.

The captain explained. "First we'll bring the rest of the men. By that time, the tide will change. Then the women and children can be rescued from the muddy creek."

The ship's rowboat prepared to go back for a second load of men. Then the captain looked up and cried out.

Over the hill and down toward the shore galloped a hundred horsemen. Again the king's troops were coming to arrest them all!

"Hurry!" the Puritans already on board shouted. "We must save the others. The soldiers must not get them!"

But the captain was already raising the anchor. "They will seize my boat! Without it, I cannot earn a living," he said. "It is all I have."

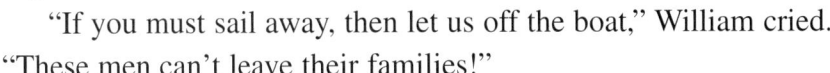

The men begged him to help rescue the others. The captain only shook his head. The sails began to fill with air.

"If you must sail away, then let us off the boat," William cried. "These men can't leave their families!"

"That would take too long," the captain said sadly. "I dare not take a chance."

Wind filled the rest of the sails. The Puritan men on board watched as the ship took them farther and farther from the English coast. They strained for a last look at their loved ones.

That night a great storm raged. Winds whirled out of the dark sky. The ship was blown hundreds of miles off course.

Things were not much better when the storm passed. Now the wind was replaced by a heavy fog. Lookouts strained their eyes for a glimpse of land.

Two days later, another storm struck. One of the worst the captain had ever seen. It lasted for seven days. The Puritans prayed continually. They never expected to see land or their families again.

At last the skies cleared. The captain steered the ship back on course. A few days later, it struggled into the harbor at Amsterdam. Now the men were in Holland.

But what about the Puritan women and children? And what about the Puritan men left on the English shore?

Before the king's soldiers could reach the beach, the younger Scrooby men and those without families ran and hid. Men with wives and children on the barge hurried to join their loved ones.

The English soldiers stopped and looked around them. What should they do now? The only prisoners they could take were grim-faced women and crying children.

By this time, the tide was lifting the barge. The soldiers had the people on board floated to the nearest town. There the Puritans were put in jail.

The jailers and the judge shook their heads. What should they do? These families no longer had homes. And most of them had no husbands or fathers to take care of them. Did the king really want to force these people to stay in England?

The judge in charge sighed. "We have no choice. Send them all back to Scrooby for now. If their husbands can pay their way, these Puritans may go to Holland."

Chapter 5

A New Start in Holland

As months passed, small groups of Puritans slipped away from England. They made their way to Amsterdam. There they joined the men from the first ship. The next year, more and more came. Finally, there were nearly 200 Puritans in the city.

But Amsterdam was a crowded, noisy city. The Puritans had lived on small farms in England. It confused them when people hurried about. And there were so many different languages!

The Puritans could read and write. But they could not find good jobs in Holland because they did not know the Dutch language.

And they could not join **guilds** because they were not Dutch citizens. So they went to work in the cloth factories.

Some wove cloth on looms. Others worked in factories where the cloth was cut and sewn into garments. None of these jobs paid well.

But the settlers had found their freedom. They could worship as they pleased. Each Sunday, they came out of their homes. They walked through narrow alleys to a meeting hall. It was an upstairs room where Catholic nuns had once lived and studied.

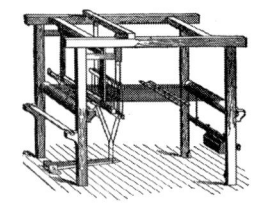

The cement walls were thick and cold. The paint was peeling. And the room was dark and damp. It was not a cheerful place to meet.

23

But the people of Scrooby didn't mind. They looked forward to gathering there all day each Sunday. At least they were free.

Once inside the meeting hall, each family separated. The men sat in one section. Their wives went to another.

Things were different for the children. A widow called a "deaconess" sat with them. She had a little birch switch to keep order. If a child whispered to a neighbor, the deaconess could reach over and sting his shoulder or ear with her switch.

Elder Brewster began the church service with a prayer. It lasted more than an hour. Everyone sat very still with bowed heads.

Then came the sermon of the day. That preaching would go on for two more hours.

How happy the children were when it was time to sing the hymns. At last, they could stand up and stomp what felt like pins and needles from their feet!

At noon, everyone walked home for a cold midday meal. To keep Sunday holy, the women would have prepared the food the day before.

The afternoon was spent quietly at home. Children did not go out to play. But young boys might be allowed to chase birds from the family's small garden.

Late Sunday afternoon, everyone went back to the meeting hall for a meeting and more prayers.

After a year in Amsterdam, a group of the Scrooby settlers decided it was time to leave.

They had heard about a smaller Dutch city, Leiden. It was known for its fine university. In Leiden, they could again find work in the wool-clothing business.

Almost 100 Puritans decided to make the move. They were happy about this new plan.

But then, all of Holland was happy in May of 1609. The mighty navy of Spain had been threatening the Dutch for many months. But now the war was ending. A truce had been signed. Peace would last for the next 12 years.

Happy years followed for the English who moved to Leiden. Again, they had the freedom of religion they had prayed for.

They did honest work and could make enough to feed their families. The English section of the city was called Green Gate. It was a good place to live.

The children were especially happy. They watched boatloads of fresh fish being unloaded on the docks. They watched windmills turn and turn, grinding grain into flour or pumping water from soggy fields.

In winter, the English joined the Dutch. They all skated happily on the frozen **canals** and rivers.

In Leiden, every child had a chance for a free education. Parents worked harder so their children would be able to spend their days in classrooms instead of in the cloth mills.

But there were worries too. Families saw their children growing away from them. Some children didn't want to keep the English ways. They didn't want to be set apart from their Dutch friends.

The older children sometimes fell in love and married Dutch young people.

Many Puritans were country folk. They missed farm life. How they longed to work with the sun on their shoulders! But they could never earn enough to buy Dutch land.

Now they spent their time in small, dark rooms. Every day they did the same dull work at their looms. Others toiled over the sewing until their eyes ached.

After 11 years, there came an even greater worry. The 12-year truce between Holland and Spain would soon end. The Dutch were preparing for war. And some of the young English boys were talking about helping to defend their adopted country.

Worst of all, if the Spaniards defeated the Dutch, everyone in Holland would be forced to follow the Catholic church. The Puritans would have no more freedom of worship than they had had under the Church of England.

After years in Holland, it was time to move again.

About that time, stories reached the Puritans of Green Gate. There was a new world across the sea. There men and women could start new farms. And they could worship as they wished.

The Leiden families listened to the stories. Was this their chance for a new start?

One day, a hardware merchant arrived from London. He and some friends were planning a settlement across the ocean.

The men from London agreed to give land to anyone who crossed the ocean and worked for the company for seven years. Excited, the Puritan families signed agreements.

The Green Gate families sold everything they had. Putting their money together, they bought a small, old sailing ship, a **pinnace.** It would carry them to England. There some of them would board a larger ship. The two ships would sail together.

The men got the ship ready for the trip. And the women of Green Gate were busy weaving and sewing for their families. Who knew when they might have new clothes again? How long before they could raise sheep to obtain more wool?

Work on their ship, *Speedwell,* was very slow. The Puritan men bought seeds for their new farms. But was it too late for a crop in the New World? Everyone was worried about that. At last in July, the small pinnace was repaired and ready.

When the Puritans boarded the *Speedwell* on July 30, 1620, they were shocked to learn they'd been tricked. The merchants they had trusted were not honest. The people of Green Gate would *not* own their houses at the end of the seven years.

But they had sold everything. Their jobs were gone. They had nowhere to live in Leiden. It was too late to turn back.

There was nothing to do but face the endless sea and the New World.

Chapter 6

A Captain Prepares His Ship

Christopher Jones stood on the deck and looked around him proudly. Yes, indeed, he was master of a sturdy ship. The *Mayflower* had served him well for 12 years.

But something else was true about the *Mayflower*. Even though Captain Jones didn't know the age of his ship, he had to admit that the 180-ton freighter seemed to be the oldest vessel there in the port of Plymouth, England. It was one of the smallest too.

For many years, it had sailed the Baltic Sea. The ship moved from one port to another in the frosty waters around Norway. Many times those seas were rough and dangerous.

But Jones was a fine seaman and a good leader. Now he faced a new challenge. Many captains would not try to cross the Atlantic Ocean in a ship so old. But Jones trusted his *Mayflower*. He was sure it would sail all the way to the New World safely.

Most of the time in the years before, the ship had carried tea or fish. Once in a while, the cargo had been lumber. Captain Jones liked the way the vessel smelled when it was loaded with fresh-cut wood.

Lately, the cargo had changed. In more recent years, the sturdy freighter had hauled barrels of wine and huge bags of spices. Those smells lingered now. Sailors liked to work on ships that had such fine smells. They called such a vessel a "sweet ship."

A breeze brought a spicy scent up from below decks. Captain Jones took a deep breath and smiled.

He was a well-respected, honest captain. And he was proud of the things he had done. Working hard, Jones had saved some money. He'd formed a company with three other men. Together, the four of them owned the *Mayflower*.

Now, as the ship's master, he faced a challenge. He must find an answer to some problems. The next cargo would be different. His orders were to carry a large group of people on his ship. And the trip would be a long one. The ship would sail across the ocean to the New World.

Where would he put 70 or more passengers? He would have to plan space for everyone. Jones was determined to do it. He and his partners needed the money the people would pay.

The ship had only one small cabin. It might hold the women and children. But the men on board would have to sleep on deck or in the hold. That would be a crowded place. Animals for food—sheep, goats, pigs, cows, and chickens—would be carried on board.

In addition, each family would bring a chest with blankets, linens, clothing, and dishes. Everyone needed kettles, pots, pans, needles, and thread. Some would have larger pieces of furniture too.

Spaces in the hold would be needed to store hoes for planting and **scythes** for clearing the farmland. They would need nets for fishing and, of course, sacks and sacks of seeds to be planted.

Life on board was going to be difficult for the passengers. But it would be as comfortable as Captain Jones could make it.

And they would need so much food! The food would be not just for the sailing but for a full year after they landed.

It was a danger. They might go hungry. It was already well into summer. It was too late to plant a crop in the New World in 1620.

Captain Jones crossed the gangplank to the pier. There were many arrangements to make. Before he climbed the hill into town, he turned to

Replica of the *Mayflower*

look once more at his fine ship. She bobbed gently at anchor there in Plymouth, England. She was a trim, tidy vessel.

Weeks later, the pier at Plymouth was piled with supplies. The men of the ship's crew, their backs bent, began carrying everything down into the hold.

Captain Jones had visited some farmers. He paid them for the wheat growing in their fields. Then he ordered the farmers to cut the wheat and grind flour. This was baked into a firm, solid bread called "hardtack." Bread like this would last a long time without growing moldy.

Then Captain Jones visited dairymen. He needed huge tubs of butter to carry on the trip across the ocean.

Meat was the next thing Jones ordered. He bought live cattle and hogs. Then he had a butcher salt and pickle the meat. That was the best way known to keep meat from going bad. The butcher filled barrels with this **salt horse.**

The travelers would need a great deal of water. Storing it was the hard part. When water was kept in barrels too long, it became **stagnant.** Stagnant water wouldn't make people sick. But it smelled bad and tasted worse.

29

The *Mayflower* had carried tea to Norway. But the English had not yet tried either tea or coffee. Those drinks might have covered the bad taste of the water.

But English people often drank beer. Barrels of beer were prepared. They were loaded onto the *Mayflower* next to the water barrels.

Captain Jones knew he would need a larger crew for this trip. He hired more sailors until there were 30 men. He also hired a *cooper,* a man to take care of the large number of barrels aboard. The cooper could also make new barrels when they were needed. Captain Jones chose a man named John Alden.

A captain had to think about danger too. Pirates could be a problem. And sometimes French or Spanish ships would attack the English. So Jones hired a man to be in charge of the military defense of the *Mayflower.*

This short, red-haired man had once been a full-time soldier. His name was Miles Standish. He prepared the two large guns on board. He also made sure the ship was loaded with helmets, steel breastplates, cutlasses, swords, and muskets.

Miles Standish

Later, both John Alden and Miles Standish would become important leaders in the New World.

At last, the *Mayflower* was loaded with food for 70 passengers and the crew. The decks were scrubbed. The sails were crisply folded, ready to be raised. The cannons in the gun room had a supply of three-pound solid shot.

It was already late August. But with good luck they would finish the trip before the winter storms.

The *Mayflower* was ready. Captain Christopher Jones waited to meet his passengers.

Chapter 7

The Voyage Is Delayed

The *Mayflower* was being prepared in Plymouth. The Puritans were on their way from Holland to England on board the *Speedwell*. Their ship would sail the mighty ocean beside the *Mayflower*. Ships sailing together had a better chance to escape the pirates that roamed the seas.

But even before the *Speedwell* reached England, her captain was worried. He could tell she was leaky and out of balance. At Southampton, England, Captain Reynolds had her carefully examined. Time was needed to plug her leaks. And the cargo was moved around for better balance.

At last, on August 15, 1620, the *Speedwell* and the *Mayflower* set out into the waters of the English Channel. Stormy weather and a rough sea slowed the ships. The *Speedwell* was only one-third the size of the *Mayflower*. She was tossed about with every wave. Then she began to leak!

Captain Reynolds signaled the *Mayflower* that the *Speedwell* was in trouble. The two ships headed for the nearest port, Dartmouth.

On September 2 after more repairs, the two ships set out again. Now the weather was good. They made steady progress for several days.

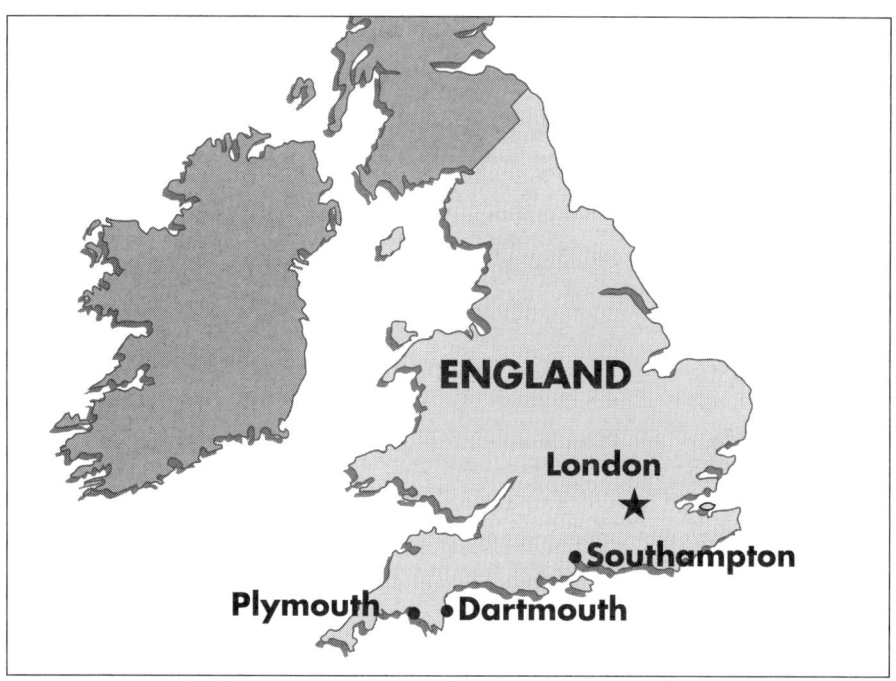

They had gone 300 miles when the *Speedwell* began to leak again. Captain Reynolds feared she would sink.

Again the two ships returned to England. This time they sailed into Plymouth, England. The shipbuilders just shook their heads. The *Speedwell* wasn't safe for an ocean voyage. She would have to be left behind.

The Pilgrims had lost seven weeks of precious time. Could the *Mayflower* make it across the ocean alone?

Eighteen passengers were ill. They offered to stay behind so the *Mayflower* could carry the others.

Thirty-five people and their belongings were moved to the larger ship. Now the heavily loaded *Mayflower* carried 102 passengers plus 30 crew. It was crowded. But at last, they could begin their voyage across the sea.

Chapter 8

Aboard the *Mayflower*

The Crossing

On September 16, 1620, the heavily loaded *Mayflower* sailed out of Plymouth, England. Her route was a northerly one. The captain hoped to avoid the pirates who stole and destroyed ships in warmer waters.

But what was that trip like? Here is a diary that might have been kept by one of the young men on board.

October 20, 1620

For this first month, the trip has gone well. We grow more used to the crowding. But there are 34 children. They have no place to run and play. And clean clothes would be welcomed by everyone.

Two of the women will soon be mothers. When the ship rolls and pitches, they are very seasick. If only the seas would calm.

October 30, 1620

We have been through many dangers on our journey. This week, in mid-ocean, a terrible storm broke over our frail craft.

Roaring winds attacked us day and night. Some of the deck seams opened. Cold, salty water poured down on those below decks. How frightened everyone was!

The storm grew worse. One of the main beams cracked. Many of us wanted to turn back to England. But Captain Jones would not hear of it. He calmed the passengers and crew. Then we repaired the damaged beam.

November 10, 1620

John Howland is a servant to the Carver family. Yesterday, he came up on deck for a bit of fresh air. Immediately, he was swept overboard. He grabbed a rope trailing behind the ship and was pulled back on board by a sailor with a boat hook. Since then, the passengers stay in their cabin and in the ship's hold.

We praise God that John is safe. And we praise Him for another reason too. A baby boy has been born to Elizabeth Hopkins. She and her husband named him Oceanus. We pray he will remain strong and healthy as we complete this trip.

December 6, 1620

After 66 days at sea, we have reached the New World. Captain Jones says we are north of our goal, but we have found a good anchorage.

The captain says we will stay here. He has dropped the anchor. Soon men will put down the small boats and explore the shore in the distance. Captain Jones wants the women and children to stay on the ship until we know the new land is safe.

Last night, Susanna White gave birth to a son. His name is to be Peregrine, which means "wanderer." It seems a fine name, for we have all wandered so far.

But at last, our long journey is over.

For 66 days, the passengers on the *Mayflower* had suffered on their journey. They were tired and dirty. Some were angry. Tempers were short.

Captain Jones was a wise man. Before any of the Englishmen could leave the ship, they signed an agreement. Each promised to stay in the settlement and work for the good of all. This agreement was the Mayflower Compact. It meant peace in the New World for the people of Plymouth.

Chapter

The Settlers Find New Friends

The Englishmen at Plymouth began to build their town. But they had many questions.

Where were the native people of the New World? Where were the ones the sea captains had called Indians? Did those people really have red skin and wear almost no clothes? Who had cleared the land here on Plymouth Bay? Why did it sometimes seem that eyes were watching from the woods?

Reconstructed seventeenth-century Plymouth

Spring came. The workers found some of their tools missing. An ax or hammer not carefully put away might never be seen again.

Then they began to catch sight of Indians in the distance. But none came close. No Pilgrim had yet met an Indian face to face.

But they had to be ready in case of trouble. It was the job of Miles Standish to see that they had protection. The leaders met with him one spring day to plan a fort. They would build it on the hill above town.

Suddenly, an Indian appeared in the doorway of their meeting house.

The March wind was blowing. But the tall man wore almost no clothes. His skin was not red. But it was a bronze color. Tucked into his belt was a small hatchet.

"Welcome," the stranger said in English.

The settlers had been reaching for their guns. They turned in surprise. Was this really an Indian who spoke English?

The native told the settlers his name was Samoset. His tribe lived to the north. "I come in peace," he promised.

"And how did you learn our language?" asked Miles Standish.

"Many sea captains have come to our shores. They catch fish in our waters and buy animal skins." He told how one of the captains had let him sail aboard his ship. Samoset had traveled down the coast to Plymouth a few months before. "I learned many more English words on that ship," he said.

The tall native visited all afternoon. He explained that the Pawtuxet Indians had lived on the cleared land at Plymouth. They had become sick, and every one of them had died. This explained the cleared land the English settlers had found along the bay.

The Pilgrims gave Samoset biscuits and cheese. They shared a bit of meat with him. When it grew dark, he showed no signs of leaving.

The Pilgrim men were alarmed! Was this Indian really as friendly as he seemed? What would happen if they all fell asleep?

One of the settlers was Stephen Hopkins. He offered Samoset a place to sleep. Mrs. Hopkins, although frightened, began to spread blankets on the ground for him.

But Samoset did not want to sleep the English way. He unrolled the skin of a deer in front of the fireplace. Soon he was sleeping peacefully.

Stephen Hopkins did not sleep that night. He believed Samoset was friendly. But still he wanted to watch and wait.

The Indian left the next morning with a knife and some jewelry as gifts from the Pilgrims. He promised to bring some men from the Wampanoag tribe, the native people he was visiting.

A few days later, Samoset returned to Plymouth. With him were five Wampanoags.

Miles Standish and the other men could hardly believe their eyes. They had thought Samoset was a big man. But these Wampanoag braves were much taller. They were almost a foot taller than Standish and the other Englishmen!

For this important visit to the settlers, the Indians had painted their faces. Streaks of yellow, red, and black stretched from forehead to chin. Each man had a deerskin over his shoulder and a bright feather in his hair.

The English settlers had very little food. But they shared it with their new friends. And the Indians showed their friendship by singing and dancing for the people of Plymouth. Then they returned the building tools that had disappeared from the town.

For days after that, the Pilgrims wondered when they would see their Indian friends again. They hoped the natives would bring fur skins to trade. This was what the investors in London were waiting for.

At last, a day came when Samoset returned with four of his friends. As Miles Standish and the other men went forward to meet them, Samoset pointed to one of the other Indians and spoke. "Squanto. He is friend to English."

The Pilgrims were amazed to hear the story of Squanto, who was also called Tisquantum. Plymouth, which had been a Pawtuxet village, was his home.

Squanto along with some other young braves had been tricked by an evil captain and taken to Europe to be sold as slaves. After nine years in England, Squanto had managed to escape. Two years ago, an English sea captain had returned him to the New World, to the northern area called Newfoundland. He had walked south for many months.

During Squanto's absence, all the people of his tribe had fallen ill and died. Squanto was the only one alive from his village. Now the Pilgrims lived and farmed on that same piece of property.

Samoset and Squanto visited the Pilgrims often in the next few weeks. They helped the Pilgrims speak with the nearby Indians about trading fur pelts for bowls, pots, and knives.

One day, the two Indians had important news for their new friends. Massasoit, the leader of the huge Wampanoag tribe, was coming to see the Pilgrims. Massasoit was bringing about 60 Indian braves with him. This could have frightened the Pilgrims. Miles Standish could have tried to scare the Indians away with cannons.

But none of this happened. Squanto ran back and forth between the Pilgrims and Massasoit, translating messages in both English and the Wampanoag language. This way, there would be no misunderstanding.

The Pilgrim leaders spread a blanket on the ground and brought seats for the Pilgrim leaders and the most important Indians. Then they gathered to make friendship plans.

Massasoit promised his tribes would not hurt the Pilgrims or steal from them. The Pilgrims promised their people would not harm the

Indians. They would help each other if either group was attacked. They would leave their weapons home when they visited. And the Englishmen promised that King James would accept the Wampanoags as his friends.

The promises made that day were important. They lasted for 50 years.

Squanto Remains a Good Friend

After the agreement, Massasoit and his men went home. But Squanto remained with the Pilgrims. There was so much he had to teach them.

Here are some of the thoughts this kindly Indian might have had.

My friends will not have food for winter unless I teach them the ways of my people. I have seen the deer traps they try to make. No animal would be fooled by those. I will show them where the animals go to drink at night and in the morning.

I will teach them to walk in the forest without making noise. To make a bear trap. To find the right berries to eat. How to call wild ducks. How to tread out the eels along the riverbank. And to make a fish trap of willow branches.

And their women must cook the Indian way. They must **parch** the kernels of dried corn and learn how to grind the cornmeal with a mortar and pestle. They must learn to build a rock fire and cover it with weeds to steam their clams. I will show my friends all these things.

Soon we must plant the corn.

Yesterday, Governor Carver saw me with a basket of the small fish called "alewives." He wanted to know why I was catching fish so very small. Today, I will show him how we plant corn.

We will go into the fields and pull up the weeds. Then we will loosen the dirt with a stick and dig holes about four footsteps apart. Each hole must have three of the alewives placed like the spokes of a wheel. When we drop corn on top of the fish and fill the hole with soil, the rotting fish will feed the growing corn plant.

Oh, there are still so many things I must teach my friends from England. If I don't, they will surely starve!

Chapter 10

Other Settlers Come to the New World

The Spaniards

Spain sent many explorers to the New World—men such as Columbus, Balboa, Coronado, and Ponce de Leon. But these men were searching for riches, not a new place to live.

Two large settlements came out of these Spanish explorations. They were St. Augustine, Florida, and Santa Fe, New Mexico.

In 1521, the Spanish king ordered Ponce de Leon to return to Florida. He was to sail to a part he had explored earlier. This time he was to begin a settlement. He landed with two shiploads of settlers. But he was killed by Indians. The settlers escaped to Cuba.

In 1565, a Spaniard named Pedro Menéndez de Avilés founded St. Augustine, Florida. It was near the spot where Ponce de Leon had landed. It is the oldest city in the United States.

Far to the west lies Santa Fe, New Mexico. It became the capital of the Spanish province of New Mexico in the winter of 1609. Santa Fe is the oldest U.S. city to have served continuously as a center of government.

Spain also held land on the west coast of North America. It was not until the 1720s that the Spanish became interested in these California lands. When Russian fur trappers began to move south from Alaska, the

Spanish government wanted to stop them. Don Gaspar de Portolá was governor of Spanish California. He and a priest, Father Junípero Serra, led expeditions north into the Indian lands of California. They built missions and changed large numbers of Indian villages into settlements.

Three French Settlements

Many of the French settlements in the New World were along the St. Lawrence River. This is now Canada. Most men who settled in that area were fur trappers. This did not bring many European families to the new area.

Some of the trappers married native Indian women and started small communities. In 1608, the French explorer Samuel de Champlain founded a settlement at Quebec.

A French Protestant group, called the Huguenots, came to Florida in 1564. They wanted to be free of the Catholic church in France.

Although the Indians were friendly to the Huguenots, the Spanish were not. They wanted to keep Florida's lands for themselves. So they drove the French away after one year.

More than 100 years later, some groups of Huguenots formed colonies in South Carolina, Virginia, New York, and Pennsylvania.

French explorer de La Salle claimed the Mississippi Valley for France in 1682. Fifteen years later, the settlers began to arrive in what became the Louisiana Territory. Two hundred colonists founded the settlement of Old Biloxi in today's state of Mississippi. By 1733, Louisiana had a population of 8,000. Most of them were French settlers.

The Dutch Settlements

Before the Pilgrims landed at Plymouth in 1620, the Dutch had built a trading post far up the Hudson River. It was in the area that had been explored for Holland by Henry Hudson.

At that time, the only settlements in the New World were Jamestown, Virginia; St. Augustine, Florida; Santa Fe, New Mexico; and the French city of Quebec.

The Dutch wanted to make money. Fur trading was the way to do it. They did not care much about settlements. In fact, the Dutch government had a great deal of trouble finding citizens who wanted to leave Holland and cross the sea.

At last, 30 families agreed to move to the New World. They were fortunate to have a fine leader in Peter Minuit.

Minuit made a famous land agreement. He traded trinkets worth about $24 with the Indians. What he got in return was the island of Manhattan. It is now downtown New York City. He called it New Amsterdam.

Unlike those in the Puritan New England communities, the Dutch welcomed settlers from other lands. Soon Swedes, French, Portuguese, and Italians had come to help New Amsterdam grow.

In 1664, four heavily armed English ships sailed into the harbor at New Amsterdam. The Dutch were ordered to turn their settlement over to the English government. Without enough soldiers to fight back, the Dutch gave up. This ended their control of what would later be New York, New Jersey, and Delaware.

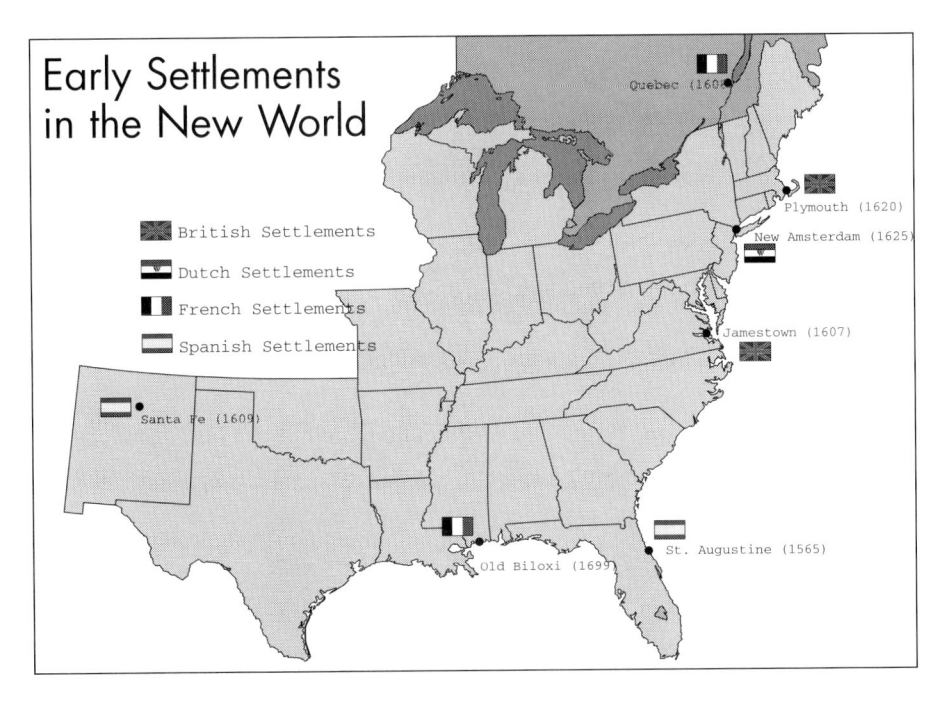

Early Settlements in the New World

- British Settlements
- Dutch Settlements
- French Settlements
- Spanish Settlements

Quebec (1608)
Plymouth (1620)
New Amsterdam (1625)
Jamestown (1607)
Santa Fe (1609)
Old Biloxi (1699)
St. Augustine (1565)

Chapter 11

The Craftsmen Among the Settlers

    The first families that came to America's shores had only the clothes on their backs. Sometimes a family had a box or chest of possessions from the old country. But there was no room on the ship for more than that.

    They needed homes to live in, food to eat, clothing, furniture, and household supplies. Many pitched in to solve the problems of the community.

    The colonial housewife prepared food and dried it for later use. She spun and wove flax to make clothing. She and her children saw to the making of candles and soap. Children gathered wood for the fireplace and water for cooking and washing.

    Men hunted and worked in the fields. When they needed objects, they made them. Soon they saw that some among them had special skills. Craftsmen began to set up work spaces and offer their services. They built their shops and factories a short distance from the town. No one wanted to smell the tannery or the paper mill.

The Wood Craftsmen

    The New World was rich in fine forests. And many of the trees were new to the settlers. But they soon learned how to make what they needed. Sometimes it was the friendly Indians who showed the settlers how different trees could be used.

Poplar wood made sturdy bowls and plates. Hickory was used to frame houses. Chestnut worked well for fences. Cedar was best for barrels, buckets, and boats. The town's carpenter used all these woods.

For farmers, the carpenter made plows, rakes, and wooden shovels. He made things for the house too. The settlers needed rolling pins, butter churns, and hoops to hold fresh-made cheese.

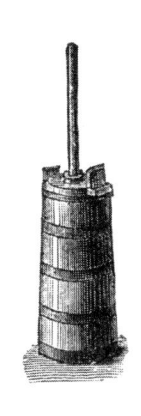

Houses were small and there was little floor space. So carpenters made furniture that could be folded and stored away when it wasn't needed. The first tables were **puncheon** logs. These long pieces of wood had hollowed out places that could be used as bowls. After dinner, the older children took the log to the nearest river or stream and scrubbed it clean for the next meal.

The settlers ate with spoons, knives, and their fingers. Napkins were passed around the family table. Then they were collected to be washed.

Because families were large, there was often no room for everyone at the table. Children stood behind the parents around the table. Parents passed food back to them.

The Potters

Soon after a new colony began, the potter set up his business. He first made bricks from the clay of the riverbank. Then he stacked the bricks to form a furnace near the water's edge.

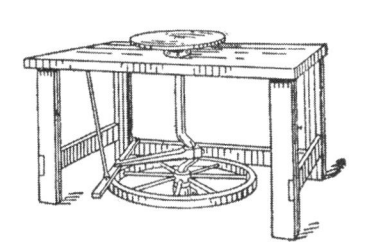

When he was ready to start his business, the potter collected soft, damp clay from the river. He pulled out the rocks and leaves inside it. When it was clean, he pounded the clay to get rid of the water.

To form the shapes he wanted, the potter "threw" the lump of clay onto a turning wooden wheel. He could keep the wheel going with his foot. His hands molded the lump of clay into a bowl or dish.

The clay was fired in the potter's furnace. It was then the color of the clay by the river. It was varnished to make it waterproof. But it was not colorful or pretty to look at.

Some settlers wanted handsome dishes with designs. If they had enough money, they could get those from England. They were delivered by a sea captain.

The Glassmakers

The settler who made glass set up his shop near the water. It might be near the potter's shop. Both men needed to build large furnaces of the special clay on the bank of the river.

At first, the glassmakers made only small colored beads to trade with the Indians. As homes were built and the town grew, they made bottles to hold ink, medicines, or oils.

Glassblowing was hard work and dangerous. If a craftsman was not careful he might breathe in some of the fumes from the molten glass. This would injure his lungs and might even kill him.

The Blacksmiths

Finally the colonies were settled in the New World. The English investors had paid the settlers' way to the New World. Now they wanted to be repaid. So products were sent to England from the New World.

One such product was iron ore. Deposits of bog iron were in the swamps near Jamestown and in some parts of Massachusetts.

In England, goods were made from the iron ore. Then the goods were sold to the colonies. With taxes added on, these goods were very expensive.

So blacksmiths in the new colonies began to make iron tools themselves. They set up workshops with great **bellows** made from animal hide. Then they built **anvils** and big stone **forges.** A steady fire burned in the forge.

People came to the blacksmith for pots and pans, wheel spokes for their wagons, and shoes for their horses. He could sharpen tools for farming or make new ones.

Some of the smaller items the blacksmith made were door hinges, gates, lanterns, and candlesticks.

The Papermakers

In the 1600s, paper was very scarce and expensive. Students learning to read and write used tree bark to practice their lessons.

There was no paper made in the New World until 1690. Then a German papermaker named William Rittenhouse set up a paper mill in Pennsylvania.

His product was made from linen and cotton rags. First he boiled them in lye and water. The rags became soft and soupy. This mixture was called *pulp*.

The pulp was poured into molds and pressed into sheets. There was never enough linen in the colonies. So paper was hard to find and very expensive.

Chapter 12

Governor Winthrop's Wonderful Tool

Rebecca, age 12, and Samuel, age 10, lived in Salem, Massachusetts. Their small village had five houses and a blacksmith's shop. Ten families lived in those five houses. The blacksmith lived in the back of his shop.

The largest and finest building in town belonged to Governor Winthrop. On one half of the first floor, the governor lived with his family. Another family lived in the other half.

A stairway led up to the second story. Most of that space was for town meetings and church services. There was also a storeroom upstairs. It held food and ammunition for the whole town.

Rebecca and Samuel were talking in the street outside Governor Winthrop's house.

Governor John Winthrop

"Father says the governor has a surprise," said Rebecca. "Governor Winthrop is going to slaughter a fat hog. We'll see the surprise when the town gathers to share the feast."

"The governor has many fine things," said Samuel. "Is this something to eat?"

"Well, no. Not exactly." Rebecca gave a little laugh. "You might say it's something to eat *with*. It's called a 'fork.' Governor Winthrop carries it with him."

"Well, a fork isn't something new," said her brother. "Father uses a fork to move the hay into Bessie's stall, doesn't he?"

"Not like that. This fork is much smaller."

"Well, Ma uses a fork to turn the meat over the fire, doesn't she?" Samuel tried again to understand. "You know, the fork with the long handle."

"Much smaller than even that one," his sister insisted. "The governor carries it in his pocket. He has a special wooden box for it."

"Why is that a special surprise?" Samuel was puzzled.

"This fork is special," Rebecca said patiently. "The governor uses it to move meat from his plate to his mouth."

"Is something wrong with his hands?"

"I don't think so. Pa says some rich people are doing that in England now. They use forks instead of their fingers when they eat."

"You mean everyone?"

"No, not everyone. In France, almost everyone uses a fork now. But not in England. You know how we English hate anything the French people do."

"But Governor Winthrop doesn't care if forks are a French idea?" Samuel asked.

"I guess not," answered Rebecca. "But I can hardly wait to see him get it out of his wooden box and use it at the feast!"

Chapter 13

The People Spread to New Settlements

In the 1630s, Jamestown and Plymouth continued to grow. Some leaders began to look for new places to settle. Some wanted less crowding. Others wanted to worship in slightly different ways.

The Puritans had adopted laws that were just as strict as those they'd run away from in 1607. People who disagreed with the Puritan ways were fined, whipped, and put in prison. Many were forced to leave the Massachusetts colony. Often they set up new settlements elsewhere near New England.

Lord Baltimore

Lord Baltimore was a title given to the Calvert family. George Calvert, the first Lord Baltimore, was a Catholic in England. But the Church of England made life very hard for Catholics. So Lord Baltimore wanted a settlement in the New World. There he would see that everyone had freedom of religion.

In 1632, King Charles granted him a charter for 12 million acres in the New World. But before the king could sign the charter, George Calvert died.

The Baltimore Crest

Cecilius Calvert

Cecilius Calvert was George Calvert's son. So he was the second Lord Baltimore. As heir to his father's charter, he settled near Chesapeake Bay. He named the area Maryland, in honor of the queen. Maryland served as a haven for English Catholics. It was a welcome settlement for those seeking religious freedom.

In 1649, the Maryland Assembly passed a law calling for religious freedom for all. From this act came one of the freedoms called for in our U.S. Constitution.

Roger Williams

Roger Williams came to the New World to preach **Separatism,** a strict form of the Puritan religion. Back in England, men who preached as he did were being hanged or burned at the stake.

Arriving in Boston, he went north to the village of Salem to start a church. He told the people they should welcome villagers of all faiths—Catholic, Protestant, Jewish, or Muslim.

The people of Salem did not like his views. They banished him. That means that they sent him away.

A friendly Indian tribe helped Williams stay alive in the forest. The tribe led him to a fine bay in what is now the state of Rhode Island. Williams bought land from the Indians. Soon his followers came to join him. Their new colony, founded in 1636, became Providence, Rhode Island.

Anne Hutchinson

Anne Hutchinson came from England with her husband and 14 children in 1634. She took care of the sick and urged the settlers to love one another regardless of their religion.

In 1637, the strict Puritans banished her from Massachusetts because of her beliefs. She moved to Rhode Island and later to Long Island in the Dutch New Netherlands. In 1643, she and all but one of her children were killed by Indians.

The Reverend Thomas Hooker

The Reverend Thomas Hooker sailed from Plymouth up the Connecticut River in 1633. Hooker was a Puritan. But he believed in freedom of worship. He also wanted everyone to have the power of a vote—not just church leaders. With 35 families, he walked for two weeks through deep forest. Reaching new land, he founded a settlement at Hartford, Connecticut.

William Penn

William Penn was the son of an English admiral. His father was often away from home, fighting wars. William wished there could be no more war!

A group called the **Quakers** wished the same thing. In 1667, William Penn joined the Quakers.

When Admiral Penn died, the king owed him a great deal of money. William talked the king into giving him a piece of land in the New World instead of the money.

Penn gathered his Quaker friends and sailed across the ocean. They settled in the new land called Pennsylvania, or "Penn's Woods." It was a hard voyage and many of the settlers came down with the terrible disease **smallpox.**

On a fall day in 1682, Penn and his friends reached the New World. Their ship sailed up the Delaware River for 100 miles. There the Quakers built a village called Philadelphia, which means "brotherly love."

James Oglethorpe

James Oglethorpe saw how miserable the poor people of London were. He asked the government for land in the New World. There he would build a colony for the poor.

In 1732, King George II granted land for Oglethorpe's new settlement. Using his own money, Oglethorpe sailed to the New World with 35 families. He bought land from the Creek Indians where Savannah, Georgia, is now. It was called Georgia, after the king.

The new colony was close to Spanish territory in Florida. But the friendly Indians helped Oglethorpe and his settlers fight to keep the Spaniards away.

Georgia meant a fresh start for poor people from many countries. Along with Englishmen came the poor from Germany and Scotland. Oglethorpe welcomed both debtors and Protestants.

Samuel Sewall

Samuel Sewall was a powerful judge in Salem, Massachusetts. In 1693, a group of young girls claimed that some residents of the settlement were witches. For three months, Sewall judged the trials of those accused. In all, 19 victims of these rumors were put to death. When the witch-hunting fever burned itself out, the town of Salem was filled with grief and shame. Five years later, in 1698, Judge Sewall admitted that he had wrongly judged innocent people.

Chapter
14

The Many Journeys of Plymouth Rock

It was 1741. And church elder Thomas Faunce had just heard the news. A new wharf was to be built in Plymouth harbor. Faunce had reached the age of 95. He spent most days in his small cozy home.

But Faunce was determined to see the town's harbor once again. He asked several friends for help. They agreed to carry him down the hill to the water's edge.

As they neared the harbor, Faunce's face lit up. "Aha," he said, "here's the big rock. My father told me that was where the Pilgrims first set foot upon the land of the New World."

No one living in 1741 had heard this story before. True, two of the *Mayflower* passengers, William Bradford and Edward Winslow, had kept careful diaries. Most of what was known about the first year in Plymouth had been learned from those diaries. But neither Bradford nor Winslow had mentioned the large rock. Perhaps it had not seemed important enough.

Now Elder Faunce was insisting that the rock was important. He said the Pilgrims used it as a pier during the first winter when the *Mayflower* was anchored in the harbor.

No action was taken until 1774. Then some residents decided the rock should be given a spot of honor in the town square. There it would serve as a liberty monument. It would be a symbol of the Pilgrims' struggle for freedom of religion. And it would be a symbol of the new struggle for freedom from English rule.

Thirty teams of oxen were driven to the waterfront. Men wrapped chains around the huge rock. As the oxen began to pull, the rock was under great strain. Suddenly, it cracked into two parts.

The top half was moved to the town square. The bottom section refused to budge and was left at the water's edge. The fame of Plymouth Rock spread. It had been deposited in the harbor by glacial action and smoothed by centuries of tidal wash. It had become both a landmark and a symbol.

In 1820, a celebration was held for the 200th anniversary of the Pilgrim landing. Orator Daniel Webster spoke of the rock as a symbol of freedom for the colonists.

Meanwhile, visitors began to chip away souvenir pieces of the rock. It was moved to Pilgrim Hall. But still pieces disappeared. The rock grew smaller and smaller. The Pilgrim Society, a history group, built a decorative iron fence around the top part of the rock.

In 1859, a new wharf was built. It crossed the lower half of the original rock. A circle was cleared in its roadway so that the rock's surface was barely visible. When visitors were expected, a city worker went to the pier to sweep away the sand and dirt. In 1867, a marble canopy was built over this spot.

Finally in 1880, the top of the rock was returned to the harbor and reunited with the bottom portion. The numerals "1620" were carved into the top to replace the painted numerals.

To celebrate the 300th anniversary in 1920, a new canopy was built. During construction, the rock was removed, again causing pieces to chip off. Because of World War I, the dedication of this new canopy was delayed until 1921.

Plymouth Rock is now one-third its original size. It can be seen today at home in Plymouth Harbor. It serves as a fitting tribute to the scores of settlers who crossed the sea to settle our country.

Permanent location of Plymouth Rock

Glossary

anvil	heavy iron block on which metal is shaped by hammering
armada	fleet of ships
bellows	instrument that blows air on a fire to keep it going
canal	waterway for navigation, for draining, or for irrigation
dysentery	disease or infection of the intestinal tract
forge	furnace where metal is heated
guild	association of craftsmen; a trade union
investor	person who gives money to someone with expectations of getting back that money and more
irrigation	means of supplying water to land that normally is dry
malaria	disease transmitted by mosquitoes; causes high fever and chills
migrate	to move from one country to another
native	belonging to a particular place by birth
parch	to dry out in the hot sun
peninsula	portion of land that juts into a body of water
pinnace	small, light sailing ship
pneumonia	disease or infection of the lungs
puncheon	split log with a smooth, flat surface
Puritans	members of a 16th- and 17th-century Protestant group in England and New England; wanted to reform the Church of England

Quakers	members of the Religious Society of Friends; known for their humanitarian activities, opposition of war and slavery, high-quality education, fight for prison reform and better treatment of mentally ill patients
salt horse	pickled meat
scythe	an implement used for mowing; a long curving blade fastened at an angle to a long handle
Separatism	religious movement that broke from the Church of England rather than trying to reform it
smallpox	a contagious disease that has oozing skin eruptions
stagnant	stale
wattle and daub	a house constructed with poles interwoven with small branches or reeds. The spaces are filled with mud.
wigwam	hut of eastern American Indians; pole frame covered with bark, rush mats, or hides

Index

Alaska, 4, 6, 41
Alden, John, 30
Balboa, 41
Baltimore, Lord, 51
Bradford, William, 18–21, 57
Brewster, William, 18, 24
Calvert, Cecilius, 5, 51
Calvert, George, 51
Canada, 6, 42
Cape Cod, 4
Catholic Church, 25, 42, 51, 52
Charles I, 51
Chesapeake Bay, 13, 51
Church of England, 18, 25, 51
Columbus, Christopher, 6, 7, 41
Connecticut, 5, 53
Coronado, 41
craftsmen
    carpenters, 13, 14, 45
    glassmakers, 46
    metalworkers, 7, 46
    papermakers, 47
    potters, 45–46
crops, 4, 7, 14, 17, 29, 40
Dare, Virginia, 10
de Avilés, Pedro, 4, 41
de Champlain, Samuel, 4, 42
de La Salle, 5, 42
De la Warr, Lord, 17
de Leon, Ponce, 41
de Portolá, Don Gaspar, 42
Delaware, 17
Drake, Sir Francis, 9
Elizabeth I, 8
England
    Dartmouth, 31
    London, 8, 9, 26, 38, 55
    Plymouth, 27, 29, 31–33
    Scrooby, 18, 19, 20, 22, 24
    Southampton, 31
English Channel, 31
Faunce, Thomas, 57, 58
Florida, 4, 8, 41, 42, 55
France, 42, 49
Georgia, 5, 55
gold, 8, 14, 16
Holland
    Amsterdam, 22–24
    Green Gate, 25–26
    Leiden, 24–26
Hooker, Thomas, 5, 53
Hopkins, Elizabeth and Oceanus, 34
Hopkins, Stephen, 37–38
Howland, John, 34
Hudson, Henry, 4, 42
Huguenots, 4, 42
Hutchinson, Anne, 5, 53
James I, 8, 14, 40
London Company, 4, 12
Louisiana Territory, 5, 42
Maine, 4
Manhattan, 5, 43
Maryland, 5, 51
Massachusetts, 5, 46, 48, 50, 53, 56
Massasoit, 5, 39–40
Mayflower Compact, 5, 35
Minuit, Peter, 43
Mississippi, 42
Native Americans
    Creek, 55
    Pawtuxet, 37, 39
    Wampanoag, 5, 38–40,

New Amsterdam, 5, 43
New Mexico, 4, 41–42
New Jersey, 43
New York, 5, 42–43
Newfoundland, 39
Newport, Christopher, 14
North Carolina, 9
Oglethorpe, James, 5, 55
Old Biloxi, 42
Opechancanough, 5, 17
Penn, William, 5, 54
Pennsylvania, 5, 9, 42, 47, 54
Pilgrim Hall, 59
Pilgrim Society, 59
Pilgrims, 5, 32, 37–40, 42, 57–58
pirates, 30, 31, 33
Plymouth harbor, 57, 59
Plymouth Rock, 57, 58, 59, 60
Pocahontas, 5, 15, 17
Powhatan, 15, 17
Puritans, 4, 5, 18–26, 31, 50, 53, 61
rivers
    Hudson, 4, 42
    Humber, 20
    James, 13
    Mississippi, 42
    St. Lawrence, 4, 42
Quakers, 5, 54, 62
Raleigh, Sir Walter, 9–10
Reynolds, Captain, 31–32
Rhode Island, 5, 52–53
Rittenhouse, William, 47
Rolfe, John, 5, 17
Russia, 4, 6, 41
Samoset, 37–39
Separatism, 52, 62
Serra, Father Junípero, 42
settlements
    Hartford, 53
    Jamestown, 4, 5, 12, 13, 14, 16, 17, 18, 42, 46, 50

Long Island, 53
Philadelphia, 54
Providence, 52
Quebec, 4, 43
Roanoke Island, 4, 9–11
St. Augustine, 4, 41–42
Salem, 5, 48, 52, 56
Santa Fe, 4, 41, 42
Savannah, 55
Williamsburg, 5, 17
Sewall, Samuel, 56
ships
    Discovery, 12, 18
    Godspeed, 12, 18
    Mayflower, 5, 27, 28, 30–33, 35, 57–58
    Speedwell, 26, 31–32
    Susan Constant, 12, 18
Smith, John, 4, 14–16
Spain, 24, 25, 41
Spanish Armada, 8, 12
South Carolina, 42
Squanto, 38–40
Standish, Miles, 30, 37–39
Starving Time, The, 16
Vikings, 6
Virginia, 4, 5, 9, 14, 42
White, John, 10–11
Williams, Roger, 5, 52
Winslow, Edward, 57
Winthrop, Governor, 48–49
witchcraft, 5, 56